SETTING THE TRUTH FREE

TRUTH FREE

ITS OK TO BE YOU EMBRACE TRANSPARENCY

I0025911

SETTING THE TRUTH FREE

ITS OK TO BE YOU EMBRACE TRANSPARENCY

Michael A. Walters, MBA

SBPC

SIMMS BOOKS PUBLISHING CORPORATION

SBPC

SIMMS BOOKS PUBLISHING CORP.

Publishers Since 2012

Published by Simms Books Publishing Corporation

Jonesboro, GA

Copyright ©Michael A. Walters, MBA 2020

Library of Congress Cataloging in Publication Data

2020903033

Michael A. Walters, MBA

SETTING THE TRUTH FREE

ITS OK TO EMBRACE TRANSPARENCY

ISBN: 978-1-949433-06-7

Printed in the United States of America

Edited by Mary Hoekstra

Book Arrangement by Simms Books Publishing

Cover by Phyllb Photography/ C. Pickney/ Urias Brown

Dedication

This book is dedicated to my family, with a special shout out to my grandchildren, my children; and to my pillars, my Mom and Dad.

To all the readers of this book who will forge their unique paths and set their truth free, we need your contributions to make the world whole!

Thanks to my photographers, Phyllb Photography and C. Pickney.

Special thanks to Mary Hoekstra, my editor.

Acknowledgments

I want to thank God most of all, because without Him none of this would have been possible.

To my rock, My Salvation, my Lord: thank You for Your Word, for it is a lamp unto my feet and a light for my path. It is by Your Word that I have the wonderful privilege to share with others and live abundantly.

I acknowledge this particular scripture by which my book is strongly influenced: Romans 12:2 "Do not be conformed to this world, but be transformed by the renewing of your mind."

Although the period of my life while I was writing this book was filled with many ups and down, writing this book about my truth was a surreal process. Writing a book has been harder than I thought, but it has been more rewarding than I could ever imagine.

None of this would have been possible without my sister Vera. She was the first to encourage me to write this book and she has stood by me through this process.

To my first love, my mother, who taught me passion, good manners, firm discipline, kind heartedness and who has given me incredible support. I thank God for allowing me to be your son.

To my dad, who showed me strength and entrepreneurial skills.

To my friends, thank you for enriching my life in so many ways. May God richly bless you all.

To all the individuals I've had the opportunity to lead and who have led me; to those whose leadership I have watched from afar, I want to say thank you for being the inspiration for the leadership Manifesto.

Table of Contents

Setting the Truth Free

Author's Note

As I communicate my new direction to more and more people, my intention becomes stronger. I want to help each of you to evoke your greatness and set your Truth free. I want to explain this new excitement that has welled up within me. Now more than ever, I want to share with you that one of the most exciting prospects about reinventing yourself lies within setting your Truth free.

Once I determined I was ready to lay aside my former identity, I set it aside, for myself and others. My former identity had me conditioned and conforming to ways that were neither comfortable nor true to me. I was in the position to decide who I wanted to become.

Now, while you are contemplating where you might go and what you might do, it is the perfect time to consider laying aside your previous roles and habits of behavior, your past ways of thinking and communicating, that have held you back from expressing your full potential. In *Setting the Truth Free,* you will discover an opportunity to let go of everything that doesn't serve you now, discover how you will live, and who you will be in the near future. Growth will only happen if we are willing to risk stretching the boundaries that have held us in our comfort zone. Stretching the boundaries of our comfort zones expands and sharpens our courage and commitment.

If *you* never set *your* Truth free:

- You will never find out what you can do.
- You will never achieve your dreams.
- You will never find out that you are much more than you ever dared to dream.
- You will never find your greatness, nor your Divinity.

Introduction

I wrote this book because I wanted every reader to understand their Truth abides in them, they have the authority to set their Truth free. Above all, I wanted everyone to fully understand that the source of our Truth -- Our Lord -- must think the world of us to have entrusted us with something so important and so powerful.

We first come to our Truth by taking the truths of others as our own. This is our "Youth Truth." It is ours, even though we cannot express it as 100% our own. "Youth Truth" comes from our conditioning, conforming, adapting, and accepting the truths in our primary environments. For example, like most of you, I had a family and an extended family environment; a community environment; a social environment where neighborhood, church and school were; and the larger environments of city, town, state, the USA, and the world.

Again, like most if not all of you, I believed that if I was good, nothing bad would happen to me. If I heard the lightning and thunder, it was just that old devil and his wife fighting.

I believed going to church every Sunday would get me into Heaven. My view of Heaven's environment was that I would go there if I was good; followed the rules; went to church every Sunday; kept The Commandments and didn't lie, steal, or disrespect my parents and elders; did what the adults in my life told me to do; cleaned my plate; shared with others; and was nice to people. I would go to hell and burn for the rest of my eternal life if I was bad, said bad words, made bad choices, and did other bad things.

The people within my primary environments exposed me to their truths, so when I was just a kid, I learned, developed, and practiced more of their environmental truths than my own. Just like you, in my youth, my truth was a result of my conditioning and conformity, both of which can be very powerful and can have significant effects on developing one's own truths. Your truth when you were a child was internalized and processed by you, but you had little control over your truth.

In no way am I even suggesting that my childhood was dysfunctional, nor that my parents were not loving. In fact, Ola Mae, my wonderful mother, is the reason why, today, I long to set the Truth free. Many summer days at the kitchen table, she would talk and she was so believable and loving that I don't think she knew she was setting her Truth free upon me... and her Truth became my Truth.

There were times when we talked and my Truth didn't always agree with hers, but of course I couldn't let her know this. But my mom Ola Mae was pretty convincing and I succumbed to her confidence because it was so clearly apparent in the manner by which she represented her Truth.

As time passed and I matured, I realized that my Truth was liberating, exciting, challenging, different and uniquely mine. This was the beginning of my becoming who I was and have come to love and respect.

Becoming yourself is my challenge to you and it is your challenge to yourself. You must set your Truth free!

Chapter 1
Borrowed Truth

I believe many of you who are reading this book can probably identify with what I call "Borrowed Truth." That is a truth given to you when you are young and it stays the same until you come of age and mature in knowing you have your own Truth. This Borrowed Truth has such aggressive, addictive, influential characteristics that it can leave a person stranded in their past state of conditioning and conformity; they can become stuck in the quicksand of believing they can never have their own truth. Borrowed Truth can linger with you from the time you were born until the time you die.

It is my desire that you will not allow this stronghold to keep you from recognizing this most sought-after phenomenon of your life: you have your Truth and you also have the ability to set it free.

In many cases, Borrowed Truth is culturally driven from within a community that has not been challenged to change, so its truth has been passed down through generations. Many times as a child I was told never to talk back, even when all I wanted was clarification and perhaps a different perspective. When I and most of you talked back, it was regarded as disrespectful. It was always, "Children should be seen but not heard." What we heard grownups say was, "Do what I say and not what I do."

Even though this kind of truth that is borrowed, provides a way of acceptance, you will want to get a clear idea of what it is before you can move toward your own Truth and grow into your purpose. Besides looking at Borrowed Truth and rules for children's behavior, it will be important to think back and discover those times when you may have touched the deepest Truth within you, when you sensed a piece of your purpose, even fleetingly.

You and I have distinctive individual talents, abilities and gifts. We are so connected to these when we are children and before they grow dim and uncertain against a barrage of, "Who do you think you are?" and "You can't do that!" and "Who said life was fair?" I think we lose track of those talents, abilities and gifts we possessed as children and long before reaching adulthood. You can never set your Truth free if it's someone else's truth, nor can Truth set you free, if you do not know your own Truth.

In this chapter, I tell you:

- Your Truth is awaiting!

- Your Truth challenges you to learn!
- Your Truth confronts you to know it!
- Your Truth invites you to claim it!
- Your Truth is powerful!
- Your Truth is necessary!

Setting your Truth free -- that Truth that is uniquely yours -- is so liberating and so exhilarating. That Truth you claim abides within you; it knows who you are and what you are doing at all times. Therefore, if Truth abides within you, then you have the authority to set it free. God has chosen and assigned you to release this Truth of yours into its own unique, amazing purpose!

This Truth within you holds the keys to your faith, spirituality, confidence, relationships, vision, your self-esteem, and your God-ordained purpose.

If you do not set your Truth free, you may find that the elements and timing of the world's truth setting *you* free can be overwhelming and devastating. If the world's truth sets you free, it will leave you feeling defeated, deserted and desperate. How often do we think so little of ourselves when we have Truth within us? For us to have this kind of power within us, and not set it free, is ridiculous! It is utter nonsense!

As I said earlier and as you know, our Truth will set us free. I'm pausing right now, reflecting on the fact that the Truth has its own time of setting us free. On the other hand, I also understand that I can set my Truth free. We will always be challenged by our conditioning and our conforming.

When you release your Truth from your conditioning and your conformity, your outcome will be your transformation. Your transformation is the result of you setting the Truth free.

Your Truth has a purpose and setting it free begins the process of you learning and knowing your purpose. Now understand, that's easier said than done. Why? Because we must understand that most of our Truth comes from conditioning and conforming, from others. So we must ask about the others in our lives, *how did they derive their truths? How were their truths communicated and taught to them?*

**Your transformation
is the result of you setting your Truth free.**

Roman 12:2 tells us, *be ye not conformed to this world but be ye transformed by the renewing of your mind.*

Truth is the core, the heartbeat and the soul of every living being that connects their Truth to the Ultimate Truth. God, the Ultimate Truth, has given you authority to set the Truth free.

It is simple: if you do not set your Truth free, God will release Truth into the atmosphere, where it will run its course. Then, nobody will know the hour nor the day their Truth will be revealed.

What I desire for all of you is that you choose the former, rather than the latter, meaning you and I have the first crack at setting the Truth free.

Think about that: when we choose to set the Truth free, it will allow us to prepare ahead of time for the outcome or the backlash that the forces of released Truth will set off!

We must consider that Truth desires to be set free so it can then set you free. When you set Truth free, it releases a moral power and an excellence of soul; it removes conformity and conditioning; and it exposes you so you can reclaim your dignity. When your Truth is set free, it releases you and empowers you to a life of enrichment and transparency.

Set Your Truth Free Before it Sets You Free

When you choose *not* to set Truth free, Truth itself will begin the process of setting you free. When Truth sets us free, the results are liberating, but the process can be very embarrassing, shameful, humiliating and hurtful.

We are exposed by Truth setting us free and even then, Truth has not finished with us. This sounds terrible I know, but Truth itself is not terrible; the process you may go through makes it difficult. You will have no control over it. In fact, that process controls you.

On the other hand, when you choose to do the work to set the Truth free, you can manage and control the process.

Chapter 2
Your Truth Will Wage
War with Borrowed
Truth

Borrowed Truth focuses on external appearances, the beliefs of others, and the wishes and ideas you have regarding your outward life. Your outward life includes lifestyle, and the importance you place on material items from your iPhone to your vehicle. You must ask yourself; *how well can I keep up my appearances?* You must also ask yourself, *is keeping up my appearance based on borrowed truth?*

Your Truth abides in and focuses on the internal you. Your Truth can include your own unique thoughts, beliefs, emotions, and behavior toward yourself and others. Your Truth is not only inside you, but it also is on your side 100%. Even if you decide to not discover your Truth, it will always be inside you, waiting for you to set it free.

Friedrich Nietzsche, a 19th Century existentialist philosopher, once said, sometimes people don't want their illusions destroyed. He was referring to "Borrowed Truth."

We all have illusions about what we should be, say, do, think, believe, and value. People who cling to their illusions are living according to their Borrowed Truth; when they begin living according to having Truth set free, the Truth will release them from such illusions. Your Truth is your foundation for living with integrity, charity, humility, faith, and purpose.

As it states in Scripture, *"when I was a child, I thought like a child, but now that I am old, I put away childish things"* (1 Corinthians 13:11).

The time has come for you to evaluate your Borrowed Truth and see it for what it really is. This is the time for you to set your Truth free.

- Borrowed Truth is a hindrance and a stronghold that never allows you to accept any of your true gifts, talents, energy, and potential.
- Borrowed Truth denies you the time to recognize and value the Truth within you.
- Borrowed Truth has such a stronghold makes such a demand on you that it will neither leave you, nor forsake you, until you demand that your Truth be set free!
- Borrowed Truth is all around you, it's in high places, in prestigious positions, in trends, lifestyles and fashions.

- Borrowed Truth seduces and entices you; its sole purpose is to drain you, but at the same time, fill you with illusions that you are free.

You are *not* free. Just as you cannot fully live on "borrowed time," you cannot live on Borrowed Truth.

Many of us have bought into a Borrowed Truth syndrome because we are selfish, lazy, weak, and easily led. We mistakenly think, *"Why should I challenge Borrowed Truth? I acquired Borrowed Truth from special people in my life, such as Momma, Daddy, school, church, community, business leaders, spouses and other very influential people in my life."*

But I get it! I know what Borrowed Truth is; I know what it does. I know it's so much easier to be what Borrowed Truth has conditioned you to become. But here I am taking a stand and I invite you to do the same.

I demand a recall on some of those beliefs and truths that were uttered to us by others. I believe you should, do that, too. You have a right to "test drive" your own Truth which you have come to know throughout your life. Your Truth will wage war against Borrowed Truth! And Borrowed Truth will battle against you and try to defeat your Truth!

Have you ever wondered or pondered or even questioned those whom you held in such high esteem? They don't encourage you or want you to attain certain positions; they don't want you to challenge their motives; and they will never accept your points of view.

Hmmm? That's conditioning; that's learning according to rewards and reinforcements by and from others. It is learning by rote, like learning to tie your shoes, learning to follow the rules in school, and learning anything from someone whose only reason for making you learn is, "Because I said so!"

Think about all the times, especially when you were a child, when someone told you to do something because "I said so," or because, "I'm your mother," or because, "That's the way we do it."

Now think about the times when your Truth defied those reasons (as we all did!) and did the opposite or didn't do what was expected. That was your Truth desiring to wage war, because it reveals what you were made to learn as

Borrowed Truths. For the most part, we went along with our conditioning and accepted what was, whether we liked it or not. That is how your Borrowed Truth conditioned you to accept the lessons, the rules, and the examples, even when your Truth desired to be set free!

Waging war means Truth is desiring to be set free. It wasn't that our "teachers" of Borrowed Truth did not realize we would question them. When we did, they would say things like, "Wait 'til you have a child, then you'll know what I'm talking about!" Or, "Wait until you start working to support yourself and your own family, then you'll see what being an adult means!" Remember, our "teachers" of Borrowed Truth most likely heard the same things when they were very young. Our "teachers" had their own "teachers!"

Your Truth wages war now because it's desiring you to set it free. It can no longer reside in the mockery, the illusions, the unchallenged realities, the "do what I say," or "don't ask questions," or "do you not know who I am?" You are at a point where you can no longer tolerate those types of precepts and concepts.

Your Truth has been waiting to exhale! It's been sitting back, holding you accountable for its breakthrough. As much as it needs you to set it free, you need it to set itself free!

Think of that! Think what your life -- and every aspect of your life-- would be like if you set your Truth free. Who could you be? Who could you become, if you won the war against your Borrowed Truth? Your truth is relentless, it is so powerful, it is so amazing, and it will bring things back to your remembrance. It will guide you, lead you, into a world of new discovery. Old things will pass away, as they should, and behold, all things will become new.

Your Truth overcomes. Your Truth is creative and innovative. Your Truth doesn't look like anyone else's, it only fits you. It is unique, like you are. No one else can have your Truth. What if you just set your Truth free and wore it like a wondrous garment?

What if you removed the habits and the patterns of the bondage of Borrowed Truth? You must unlock the stronghold of Borrowed Truth because Borrowed Truth delights in seeing you never come into the knowledge of your purpose. Borrowed Truth continues to lead you along a path that has only a demonstrated outcome of unhappiness, uncertainties. Borrowed Truth leaves you always second-guessing yourself.

Have you ever realized that you were not living your life but implementing the script written by someone else? I often think that Borrowed Truth's intentions are to create so much disharmony and discord and to sustain them over a long period of time, that you will never establish your Truth, nor set your Truth free.

Truth has been given to you by God to influence you, to guide you, and how to guide your interpretation of how people have revealed their truth to you. When your Truth is set free, it releases and empowers you to a life of enrichment impacted by God!

The truth reveals pains. Truth will lead you. Truth is wisdom, guidance, appreciation, love, power. Outward Truth must be fed to your inner Truth.

Chapter 3
Transformational
Conditioning

Your transformational conditioning reflects your traits of honesty, courage, openness, vulnerability, and anything else in you that is less than perfect. Your Truth will not allow you to be so hard on yourself, but it will allow you to appreciate your most illuminating qualities. Your unique inner attractiveness or worth then transforms itself into your outer attractiveness.

Conditioning entices you to believe that everybody else is so together on the outsides and so smooth, that if any difficult, uncomfortable or painful feelings come up, you define them as wrong and bad; you pretend nothing is wrong and everything is lovely.

That is a common falsehood we convince ourselves is true. Your Truth will reveal to you what is broken and fractured within yourself. Your Truth will reveal your imperfections, because it knows you are conditioned to hide your struggles and the parts of yourself that you think are flawed.

I talk with lots of people and I've noticed the same trends:
- how some people express that their lives are so perfect; how some people travel from place to place;

- how some people's children are doing wonderfully; and
- how their own lives seem to be perfect.

I like knowing that, but it's also good to meet genuine people who don't want to be envied; they just allow their Truth to reveal their conditioning, their experiences and their lives with openness, without lying about what they have and how much more they will get.

Conditioning is not inherently bad, but if you allow it to control your habits and patterns and control your thoughts, it creates an inner challenge, especially if it goes against your beliefs and your inner Truth. Conditioning that is controlling can so inundate you and overwhelm you that you become unaware how it is leading you down a path where you do not want to permit yourself to go.

Conditioning results in conformity. Unless you are aware of your conditioning, your conformity to it becomes absolute. You must be aware of your environment, friends, leaders, and influential people you admire or emulate. Why? Because we are all creatures of habit. We can create our own habits, too. We can reveal transformational conditioning by renewing our minds and becoming transformed beyond our unique experiences. (Roman 12:2)

This transformation is your Truth. Upon your transformation, you are entitled to condition your own, unique, true way of thinking; your way of understanding; your interpretation of everything you perceive; and your expressions of how you feel. You have the right to ask any question without feeling intimidated.

This transformational conditioning will shatter the myth that people will do whatever it takes to have it all together. Transformational conditioning leads you to question why you are spending valuable time and energy striving for unrealistic and impossible goals. Transformational condition will refresh you with new boldness, so you, like Adam and Eve, can be naked but not ashamed! You would not be afraid to let someone know where you are in life.

Transformational conditioning helps you stop focusing on whether someone likes you or not, or whether they will accept or reject you. You would have no need for such questions from within yourself. Quite frankly, transformational conditioning is unfamiliar territory to many people, as well as to you, but it dwells within you; it is your Truth. Until you wage war against your Borrowed Truth and your own conditioning, you will lack courage and might be easily intimidated.

Broad is the way that leads to destruction and many enter through it; however; narrow is the way that leads to life and few find it. (Matthew 7:13)

It is obvious that many of us choose not to act because we are at a point in our lives when changes don't seem necessary; we just continue to maintain our own status quo. I know, without a doubt, that if you have read this far, you are reflecting and re-positioning yourself for your own transformational conditioning and your own Truth.

Transformation conditioning helps you let your light shine so that everyone can see your good works. When you bring about transformational conditioning inside yourself, you will open up and admit your flaws and struggles. That is the time for you to rejoice in the way you can set your Truth free!

Chapter 4

Your Experience Truth

Often, we don't take to heart the experiences we encounter. More often than not, we have overlooked our experiences and depended instead upon the severity we would rather not have. I have come to understand that the most important asset or gift I have been given is the sum of all my experience.

My experience has guided me, brought things back to my remembrance, and taught me valuable lessons. My experience has taught me to not repeat the same mistakes.

Your experience is your Truth and how you interpret your experience will determine how your "Experience Truth" can be of tremendous value to you. Sometimes, your Experience Truth cannot be shared with others simply because your experiences can come to you in ways that only you can know. It's your responsibility to determine the significance of your experiences and why you have them.

Often, we are uncertain of the meaning of our experiences and we do not know why certain experiences are good and some are bad. Regardless of those questions, the experiences you encounter represent a Truth and should not be overlooked, forgotten, nor under estimated. Your experiences are powerful, full of potential; each is a gift that is often unappreciated, regardless of how painful it may be. Your experiences are full of energy; creativity; imagination; humor; wisdom; and are your unique information packed with your own Truth.

I am convinced that your Experience Truth is ready to be set free, to be shared with someone who has kept their experiences in hiding and shame, someone who has been reluctant to share. If your experiences have not been set free, how can you set the Truth free?

Think about your life and the many experiences you have encountered. Think about how you only accepted those experiences that were acceptable to others. Your experiences should take you into unfamiliar territory and allow you to take in all the ups and down, bumps and bruises, hurt and pain, the good and the bad; you must see them as blessings, rather than an enemy attack upon you.

The purpose for your Experience Truth is not geared for the present but rather for future encounters. You must understand that what you experience will properly position you against persuasions that your experiences have neither proved nor disproved.

The experiences of your Truth are a remarkable, free gift the Almighty gave you. The characteristic of experiences is very similar to what is spoken in the Gospel of John, 16:12-14: *Howbeit when he, the Spirit of Truth is come, he will guide you into all truth; for he shall not speak of himself; but whatsoever he shall hear, that shall he speak; and will show you things to come.* (KJV)

Out of your experiences you can find the True You, your passion, your forgiveness, and you can discover love. Out of your experiences, you can remove conditioning, you can become an informed leader. Then there will be nothing to separate you from the True You, because you would have found the True You through your very own experiences. Your experiences are your Truth and are a barometer or a measuring mechanism that will let you know how far you have come.

Neither take your experiences lightly, nor for granted. Many of you don't appreciate your experiences and never learn from them. There are countless consequences and repercussions that await you and those whom you encounter.

It has been said, "Some things should be kept within," however, your experiences should be transparent and should have the freedom to speak volumes and to transcend beyond your perspective. You should have the right to interpret what happens to you in your darkness by your light. Your light should shine from experiencing your Truth.

The immeasurable teaching that your experiences teach you may cause others to be mindful of you, envious, full of critiques and ridicule, and sometime may make you feel like an outcast, and may even inquire about your way of thinking as a way of alternative resolution. If that is the case, you are setting your truth free. Yesss!

It's okay to be you! Your experiences are different, your understanding of your experiences is different. How you interpret your experiences is different. You are different and that's fine, if you just learn to recognize the full worth of Setting Your Truth Free from your own Experiences.

Every day, valuable experiences present you with opportunities to gain insight that will either validate your truth with your experiences or will inform you of others' truths that are suspect according to your experiences. Your experience is essential to the process of "Setting Your Truth Free."

Chapter 5

Achievement Truths

You must personally manage your Truth. Achievement Truths are about being successful. Although success comes in many different forms, it is never guaranteed but must be earned. Your Achievement Truth is about responsibilities, about what you have done for yourself lately. You must grow into your responsibility of setting your Truth free You must gain control of your own life and overcome day-to-day challenges.

Being responsible is acting according to Your Inner Truth and listen to your True Self. No one else can fix your life but you. Napoleon Hill (1883-1970) once said, "The greatest achievement is usually born of great sacrifice and is never the result of selfishness."

https://www.brainyquote.com/quotes/napoleon_hill_152870

Your destiny is your own responsibility. Fear and laziness are conditions brought on by those who can't handle tough times because they see everything around them as painful and directed towards them. God has not given us a spirit of fear therefore, we must believe it to achieve it. You must be willing to create your own success. As Scripture tells us, *Be strong and very courageous, focus, be not afraid nor in distress; this way leads to success.* (Joshua 1: 7, 9 KJV)

Only you can change your thinking patterns. You are the only one who can change your mind. God can empower your mind but you must empower your will. The toughest challenge for you is the length of time you spend in the conditioning phase of your wilderness. What you hear and what you see are minor, compared to what you think.

As a Man thinks in his heart, so is he. (Proverbs 23:7)

The choices and decisions you make every day represent the total truth of who you are. Your attitude about your mind can and will delay your progress. Once you free your mind from those whose intentions are to control you or oppress you, only then can you experience a transformation and a mighty movement from God.

It's not what you are that holds you back, it's what you think you are not.

Ask yourself how successful your journey has been and why it hasn't gone to the next level. There are so many of us struggling and traveling aimlessly from place to place. So many of us are doing less than what is expected in our aggressive and fiercely competitive world, because our information doesn't bring about transformational conditioning.

Within you is your potential Achievement Truth Space that is directly tied to setting your Truth free. You have control of that potential, so there are things to do and things to not do. Don't let thoughts just roam freely within you, control them; be attentive and aware of what thoughts are occupying your potential Achievement Truth Space. Make them accountable and determine whether they are responsible; if they are not, release them from your Achievement Truth Space. You are the author and finisher of your achievement. Your Achievement Truth demands that you be responsible, accountable, self- confident, consistent, determined, and disciplined. You must be able to prioritize and organize. You must fuel your Achievement Truth with those proven remedies that will launch you into a state of mind that permits you and frees you to do all things.

This mindset is necessary; you should not fear it, nor allow anyone to make you think otherwise. Your Achievement

Truth understands its positioning and its authority. It only allows those who:

- are relentless;
- have been tested and tried;
- are sick and tired of being sick and tired;
- no longer desire to be conditioned;
- no longer allow themselves to be held back; and
- will no longer allow themselves to be in bondage.

Achievement Truth symbolizes where you've come from to where you are. Achievement Truth tramples Borrowed Truth. Conditioning no longer has any purpose but is only ramshackle oppression that reminds you of your transformation (deliverance), your independence and your strength on your way to setting your Truth Free.

Achievement Truth has your name written all over it and assures you that you can do all things with the right resources and tools God Almighty made and continues to make available to you.

Don't let your past interfere with your future. Those of us who are Achievers of Truth understand the past is just that; we know we can't change the past. We understand we will determine the quality of our future by setting the Truth Free.

I am excited for you and you should be, too. You have read this far and now you are about to take responsibility for your success.

Never hesitate. It is never too late to set your Truth Free, regardless of how old or how young you are. You need your success, not only for you, but also for those who don't know that they need you. Attaining Achievement Truth is why you should set your Truth Free.

Chapter 6: The Ultimate Truth Is Within YOU

The only road to setting your Truth free starts with your power of self-discovery in the Ultimate Truth. You have the power to believe in yourself and to believe that "greater is He that is in You." So the tools and roadmap are there.

What other people believe about you is not important. What's important is only what you believe about yourself.

The one who knows the Truth about you is You. Your entire experience in life is fabricated upon what you believe about yourself. And let me remind you, what other people believe about you is not important. What's important is only what you believe about yourself. You must be the kind of person you can believe in. Think of a person you know and believe in now, or someone you knew and believed in before. You must have those same high standards to believe in yourself: honesty, self-worth, respectability, and decency all are necessary for you to set the truth free.

You may ask, "What about believing in God?" Please hear this answer: your Faith is no good until you learn to have faith in yourself. How can you believe in God in His Heaven when you can't believe in yourself? How can you believe in a Jesus who walked in Galilee and not believe in a God who walks in you?

It doesn't matter how much Faith you have in a God in the sky until you learn to have Faith in the God within you. Your Faith is dead; it is useless because the God in the sky is useless to you. Only the God in you is of any value to you.

There are some religious people who will tell you that you should not believe in yourself, but you should believe in God. My question to them is, "Where do you think God resides?" He resides on the inside of you. God has no personality except in man and as man. God is not the big illusion of a man in the sky, He is the Real Deal that is in you.

Repeat after me: "God is not an apparition, He is not an illusion, He is the true God who resides in me."

Right this moment, God is the presence and power of you. God is the Creator, the Mastermind, the Ultimate Truth working through you. I believe, once you learn to truly believe in yourself, you no longer need to worry about what other people think or say about you. Unless you learn to believe in yourself, you will not be able to move up, move ahead, and move past where you are now. Maybe you'll take a small step, but you won't get far.

You must come to that point in your experience when you know your nose is clean; your business is straight; you know that it's tight but its right; and you don't give a damn about what other folks do or say.

Excuse me, Saints, did I say that?

The thing about people is, they don't want to change their thinking, they don't want to change their minds. People want to change everyone and everything *except* themselves. People know exactly what everybody ought to do, but they don't know what the hell they ought to do.

Now someone may ask, "How does God work in me?" God works in you and for you from within your very own mind. When you get ahold of your own mind and of yourself, then God in you will lead you, guide you and direct what you do.

It's funny how people know what God ought to do; people tell God what to do, including telling God to change this person, change that person. Those same people do not want to change their negative thinking, or admit they are powerless to tell God to do anything!

So many places in the Bible, you'll find, "believe." Each time that is mentioned, it means for you to believe in yourself, believe in the presence of God in you, believe in the power of God in you.

When the Bible mentions, "believe in the Son of God," it means to believe in yourself. You must use your mind to believe you can be and you can do whatever you desire. The first step to achieving your desire is to believe you can!

So-called "religious" people have the worst hang ups. They pray and say, "Lord I am not worthy," or, "Lord I don't deserve your goodness." That's incredible; it makes me laugh, but now shout if you have said this type of prayer, because I believe we all did at one time or another.

Believe you deserve to have the good you desire, that you are worthy of all God's goodness. You don't have the right to ask someone else to believe in you if you don't believe in you. Use your Ultimate Truth to set you free, decide what you want and those things will have no other choice but to manifest themselves to you. God delights in giving you the desires of your mind. The Ultimate Truth is believing in the God within you.

Setting the Truth free is your way of expressing the liberty that God has given you; it is your recognition that God has granted you permission to become anything that you choose to be. The Ultimate Truth provides you with all the confidence and the strength you need to overcome any conditioning or habits that are not beneficial to you, nor to anyone.

Setting your Truth Free is essential to your success and to your spiritual walk; once you take that step, old things are passed away and you will enjoy the newness of life.

Setting your Truth Free
Exercises and Questions

1.   What are some Borrowed Truths that you still hold onto today but should let go?

_____

_____

_____

_____

_____

_____

_____

_____

_____

_____

_____

_____

_____

_____

_____

_____

_____

_____

_____

_____

_____

_____

2. **How have your experiences in life became your Ultimate Truth?**

_____
_____
_____
_____
_____
_____
_____
_____
_____
_____
_____
_____
_____
_____
_____
_____
_____
_____
_____
_____
_____
_____
_____
_____
_____

3. How do you know if you are truly ready to change your life, to take hold of that Freedom you've been missing? What are two things you need to do?

_____
_____
_____
_____
_____
_____
_____
_____
_____
_____
_____
_____

4. Why are you not connected to your real Truth, but you're connected instead to your delusional emotional self-talk?

_____
_____
_____
_____
_____
_____
_____
_____
_____
_____
_____
_____
_____

5. **Which of these bests describes where you are in setting your Truth free? What are you currently doing about it? Choose all that apply and write your reasons.**

A. I am led by my emotions.

_____
_____
_____
_____

B. I let my internal condition control the quality of my life.

_____
_____
_____
_____

C. I sell myself out or sell myself short.

_____
_____
_____
_____

D. All of the above

_____
_____
_____
_____

E. Other

_____
_____
_____
_____
_____

Things to ponder: Truth Setting when you know the difference.

1.What is the difference between Truth and Facts?

_____
_____
_____
_____
_____
_____
_____
_____
_____

2. Everything about your life is now in your own hands. How is that so?

_____
_____
_____
_____
_____
_____
_____
_____
_____

3. Thinking and doing are not the same thing. Please explain.

_____
_____
_____
_____
_____

4. Are we all born equal?

_____

_____

_____

_____

_____

5. Do you believe people do judge a book by its cover?

_____

_____

_____

_____

_____

Your notes:

_____

_____

_____

_____

_____

_____

_____

_____

_____

_____

_____

_____

_____

_____

_____

_____

_____

www.ingramcontent.com/pod-product-compliance
Lightning Source LLC
Chambersburg PA
CBHW070932280326
41934CB00009B/1837